# Fun Facts About Dogs

## Inspiring Tales, Amazing Feats, and Helpful Hints

### Written and Illustrated by
### Richard Torregrossa

BARNES
&NOBLE
BOOKS
NEW YORK

This book is dedicated to
Gridley, a dog like
no other.

# Acknowledgments

I would like to thank my friends Ken and Justine Wenman for their help and encouragement; Carolyn Harmon, a cheerful and extremely competent researcher who zips around the World Wide Web like nobody else I know; the pet-loving and hard-working people at Health Communications, Inc.—Peter Vegso, Christine Belleris and Allison "I'll Send it FedEx" Janse. Thanks also to Lawna Oldfield and Sandy Brandvold for their creative and thoughtful graphic design.

Also, to Steven Kent, my literary and art agent, whose guiding light is always there—except when he's in London working with other clients.

# Preface

One day when I was ten this black-and-white dog showed up on our doorstep and refused to leave. She was a mixed-breed corgi with short muscular legs and a long frankfurter-like body. While most pet owners adopt their pets, this dog adopted us. She sat on our front porch like a sentry, barking at every stranger who walked by. And she wouldn't leave. We had no idea where she came from nor did any of our neighbors. It was as if she had been divinely assigned to our residence. So we had no choice but to accept her into the family.

She remained with us for the rest of her life, through some good times and through some very, very bad times. She was so ferociously protective of each

member of my family that the neighbors complained, so my father took her to work with him. He owned a store in Brooklyn that sold and repaired televisions. This was in the early '70s, in the days when televisions ran on cathode-ray tubes.

One day while he was testing tubes on a big machine the dog jumped up and started barking. My father said, "Be quiet." Reading the tube meter, he added, "Ah, gridleak!" Gridleak was a technical term for a burnt-out tube. Somehow the term got connected to our dog. So that's what we called her, until it was shortened to Gridley.

Gridley slept at the store—"guarding it" as my father explained, but my sister and brother and I didn't buy it; after much pestering, Gridley was brought back to the house.

I didn't realize then what I realized while I was writing and illustrating this book: Gridley was an extra-ordinary dog. I've never seen or heard of another dog quite like her. She would scratch on the door when she wanted to go out, and scratch on it again when she wanted to come in. Wherever we went, she followed. One morning when my mother was driving us to school

in our old yellow Corvair, we looked behind us: There was Gridley running at full tilt, hot on our trail.

She soon became something of a neighborhood legend—or a colossal scourge, depending upon your point of view. She chased not only cats, but cars, motorcycles and bicyclists too. She growled and threatened strangers she didn't like.

Yes, we should have had her on a leash, but Gridley was an independent dog, a free spirit. Our neighbors didn't agree, especially the ones she chased down the block. She was as much hated as she was loved. More than one attempt was made to poison her with tainted hamburger meat, but Gridley outsmarted her enemies. She contemptuously turned up her nose at the poisoned vittles and went right on terrorizing roller-skaters and anyone else she regarded as "trespassers." Complaints were made to the ASPCA, but she was never captured because we hid her under our bed.

In the vacant lot across the street from our house where we played football, Gridley played too. She'd bite the laces of the football and run like the wind for a touchdown; nobody could catch her. When I was sick, she would sleep with me. When my sister or brother was sick, she'd snuggle up with them.

She is warmly present in almost every memory I have of growing up. She died of old age many years ago, but she outlived my father, and my parents' marriage.

Last Christmas I went back to the red-brick house where I was raised, the house that is now inhabited by some other family, the house we haven't lived in for almost twenty years. The awning I helped my father install is still there; so is the plaque that bears the address, "1500 East 46th Street." The house is eerily unchanged. I almost expected, hoped, to see Gridley's ghostly presence sitting on the front steps, a guardian angel dutifully at her post.

But of course that's all changed. There was no sign of her. What's left of her remains only in our hearts and memories. Our family is no longer together the way it once was, but we still talk about Gridley, the dog that left such a happy mark on our difficult lives.

*Richard Torregrossa*
*San Diego, California*
*April 1998*

# Fleet-Footed Fido

If you've ever seen a dog chase a cat, then you know dogs can run like the wind. But just how fast are they? Most domestic dogs are capable of reaching speeds of about nineteen miles per hour when running at full throttle, but the members of the greyhound family are the fastest; they're able to reach speeds of up to forty-four miles per hour.

## Can You Hear Me?

A dog's hearing is superior to that of humans, espe-cially for high-pitched sounds. Canines can hear sounds that are ultrasonic. If a dog suddenly pricks up its ears and becomes alert for no apparent reason, he might have detected bat or rodent sounds that are inaudible to us.

# Top Dog

The Saint Bernard is the heaviest breed of dog, followed by the English mastiff, Great Dane, Irish wolfhound, Tibetan mastiff and the Newfoundland.

# Heroic Dog Turns
# the Tide of History

There are many stories about dogs who have hero-ically rescued their masters from perilous circum-stances. But probably the incident with the most historical significance occurred in 1815, when Napoleon was returning to France after his exile on the island of Elba. As he paced the docks, waiting to be taken to the

ship that would deliver him to the mainland, he slipped and fell into the sea. A Newfoundland on a nearby boat leaped in after him, chomped down on his collar and towed him to safety.

Had this brave dog not acted so decisively, perhaps that would have been the end of Napoleon—and Waterloo, one of history's most famous battles, would never have taken place.

# Dog Lover with a Big Heart—
# And a Lot of Extra Room

Dog lovers frequently own more than one dog, but the record for owning the most dogs belongs to the thirteenth-century emperor Kublai Khan, grandson of Genghis Khan. He owned a grand total of five thousand mastiffs, give or take a few pups.

# Dogs Take a Licking

Dogs have many curious habits. First among them has to be the tendency to lick their most private parts. Although it might seem perverse, it serves an important purpose. The dog's genitourinary tract will not function without the stimulation that comes from frequent licking.

# Small Dogs Are Here to Stay

Small dogs live the longest. Toy breeds live up to sixteen years or more; larger dogs seven to nine years.

On average, a dog's life span is about twelve years, but advances in veterinary medicine have extended this estimate by about three years. However, some breeds, like the Tibetan terrier, live as long as twenty years.

# Good Luck Dogs

In many cultures, dogs are considered powerful good-luck charms with the ability to ward off demons. In ancient China, for instance, the sentinels responsible for guarding the imperial court dressed in canine costumes and barked away evil spirits.

# Is It Night Yet?

In ancient Rome, dusk had officially passed into night when one could no longer tell whether a canine in the distance was a dog or a wolf.

# Feeding Tip

Dogs that are fed a regular diet of dried dog food are often thirstier than those fed canned or moist foods. This is not because dry dog food is saltier, but because there is less liquid in the dry vittles than in other forms of nourishment. So make sure that your dog has plenty of clean, fresh water.

# Heel, Comrade!

In Russia, the most popular dog names are taken from the names of canines who have traveled into space. Ugoljok (Blackie) and Veterok (Breezy) are two of the most common monikers.

# Why Do Dogs Howl?

City dogs are often left alone for long periods and howl because they are lonely. The purpose of the howl in the wild, however, is to gather the pack so that they can face impending danger together. The group howl is also a kind of tribal bonding experience.

# Dogs and the Rain

Dogs often hesitate before venturing into the rain. It's not because they're afraid of getting wet, but because the rain amplifies sound and hurts their sensitive ears.

# Mel Gibson, a Supermodel or Spot?

If you were stranded on a deserted island without cable television, who would you pick to keep you company? It's a tough choice—unless you're a pet owner. According to the American Animal Hospital Association, most pet owners prefer a kitty or a canine castaway to a human companion.

More than half of the 1,019 pet owners surveyed would prefer to be with their pet even when given the choice of actor Leonardo DiCaprio or supermodel Cindy Crawford.

# Porky Dogs

One dog in four is fat. These chubby canines fall into the same lifestyle pitfalls as their owners can—they eat too many snacks and high-fat foods, and don't exercise enough. This is undoubtedly a consequence of domestication. Obesity is unheard of in the wild. Overweight dogs are more likely to be ill and don't live as long as trim ones.

Here's how to tell if your dog is a porker. Feel its ribs at about midchest level. Gently glide your fingers over this area of your dog's body. A thin layer of fat is normal. However, if you can't feel the ribs, your dog is too fat.

Check with your vet first, though, before putting your dog on a diet.

# Work (Out) Like a Dog

Dogs need—and enjoy—exercise, especially if they're putting on the pounds. Experts recommend that dogs get regular exercise about three times a week, which should include walking or running. This will increase the metabolic rate of canines just as it does humans, allowing them to burn more calories and maintain a healthy weight.

But don't overdo it. Dogs are so loyal they will run alongside their masters way past the healthy point. In fact, they'll run until they drop dead from exhaustion. So keep a look out for signs that your dog is tiring, such as excessive panting or salivating, a labored stride, a reluctance to continue, or sudden stopping. Some dogs get a glazed look in their eyes.

For a greyhound, a mile is a piece of cake when they are fatigued; for a bulldog it's a long way. Be aware, then, of your dog's level of fitness so that you don't push beyond its limits.

Be aware, too, that if your dog isn't exercised regularly, a vigorous workout might do him more harm

than good. His lack of muscle tone can make him more prone to injury, especially in the knees and back.

For a dog who is physically fit, the beach is a fun place for a run or a walk; but just make sure he doesn't drink the salt water (it'll cause diarrhea). And if you're up for a game of fetch, throw only soft Frisbees and balls to avoid damaging your dog's teeth.

# Dogs in the Military

During World War I, Airedale terriers worked twelve hours a day on strict rations carrying messages to and from the front line.

# It's a Bird, It's a
# Plane—No, It's an Airedale!

During World War II, dogs were once again con-scripted into the military to do their part. Airedales, a breed of large terriers with a hard, wiry coat that is dark on the back and sides and tan elsewhere, were parachuted behind enemy lines by the British army to accompany raiding parties and to help spy missions.

The name "Airedale," however, derives not from their peculiar relationship with the air, but from the fact that they were bred about a hundred years ago in Yorkshire, England, in the valley of the Aire River.

Airedales became paratroopers because they were inexpensive, faithful to those they knew, suspicious of strangers, and possessed good hearing and scenting skills.

# A Dog's Nose Knows

The canine nose works 1 million times more efficiently than the human nose, but only for smells that are of doggie importance—like barbecued steaks and meatloaf. The fragrance of flowers, on the other hand, registers only faintly.

Some dogs, however, have better noses than others. According to the North American Police Work Dog Association (NAPWDA), the ability to sniff out suitcases filled with drugs is more a matter of talent than innate ability. NAPWDA tests its dogs, and only those with the best performance scores are hired.

# Why Do Dogs Pant?

Since they only have sweat glands on their feet, dogs cannot lose heat rapidly by perspiring from head to toe the way humans do. Instead, dogs "sweat" by panting, which removes body heat by evaporation from the surface of the tongue.

Dogs also pant when they are nervous or excited—a way for them to "cool down."

## Don't Eat the Snow—
## Yellow or Otherwise

It's always fun to run and play with your dog in the snow, but eating snow, no matter how clean or pure, is not good for your dog. It causes spasms in the gastrointestinal tract, which can lead to diarrhea, stomachaches and colds.

# Why Does a Pointer Point?

This behavior comes from the wolf, of which the dog is a direct descendant. When the lead wolf in a pack smells its prey, it freezes and points itself in the direction of the scent. This gives the other members in the pack a chance to pick up the scent, too. There is a pause before they are all in unison; it is this wolf pause that the pointer dog is imitating.

# Dogs Love to Be Loved

Studies show that a lovingly handled dog is a healthier dog. The touch of the human hand improves the function of virtually all of the sustaining systems: respiratory, circulatory, digestive, and so on, in newborn puppies. A frequently petted puppy is not only healthier and happier, but also better behaved.

Dogs, like humans, find solace in touching another living being, which is another reason why they get along so well together.

# Why Do Dogs Bark?

Barking is often a canine alarm. Its purpose is to let people as well as other dogs know that something—whether that be an approaching intruder or a stray—is trying to encroach upon territory it regards as its own.

In the wild, barking tells puppies to take cover and hide, and also alerts the other dogs in the pack to assemble for action. An out-and-out attack by a dog, however, is silent.

Dogs also bark because they're bored, anxious or excited. Sometimes the reason is purely physical—they're hot, cold or hungry.

# A Dog with
# Bite But No Bark

If you love dogs but hate the sound of barking, here's a possible solution—a barkless dog. The basenji, from the Congo, is a breed of dog that does not bark but instead makes a yodel-like sound.

# How Many Dogs Are There?

There are 150 million dogs worldwide; 40 million in this country.

In the United States, the Southwest is the area with the most dogs. And California, boasting a population of 5.7 million dogs, is the state with the most canines.

# Why So Many Dogs?

During the industrial revolution, dogs were bred for specific purposes. Sheepdogs, hunting, attack and guard dogs are a few examples of "working dogs."

Deliberate breeding was so successful that more dogs were bred than were needed. This, combined with the dog's natural tendency to procreate, resulted in a surplus of dogs.

# Man's Best Friend—But Why?

It is probably because dogs are incredibly loyal. There are many stories on record testifying to this fact. One of the most impressive took place over a century ago in England. A terrier named Bobby was so devoted to his master that after his master passed away, he sat by his grave every day for fifteen years in Greyfriars Churchyard.

# Happy Holidays, Rover

Eighty percent of dog owners buy their pooch a present for holidays and birthdays. More than half of them sign letters and cards from themselves and their pets.

# How to Calculate Your Dog's Age

The old formula for obtaining the age of your dog was to multiply every year of a dog's life by seven human years. But that's not accurate. A dog is full grown at twelve months, which would be age eighteen in human terms. From this point on, to calculate the true age of your dog, figure that every dog year is the equivalent of five human years.

Thus a ten-year-old dog is sixty-three years of age in human terms, calculated this way: The first year of a dog's life counts as eighteen; then add five years for every additional year. Since there are nine additional years, add forty-five to the eighteen to arrive at sixty-three.

My Dog is 52 yrs. old?

# Is Your Dog Telepathic?

Maybe. If you're one of the many dog owners who often get the feeling that your dog can read your mind, that could be exactly what she's doing.

In Russia, a team of doctors and scientists conducted 1,278 telepathic experiments with dogs, of which 696 were successful. Most of the experiments involved testing the dog's ability to read unspoken

commands. The research team concluded that some ESP factor must be at work.

"It was mathematically preposterous," writes Dennis Bardens in *Psychic Animals*, "to suppose that dogs could, in more than half the unspoken commands, have responded correctly merely by chance. It would be tantamount to a human being backing every second number correctly on a roulette wheel.... The odds against this would be billions to one."

# Dogs as Healers

The relationship between man and dog is a special one. It is no wonder, then, that more and more health-care practitioners are recommending that their patients adopt a pet to help them through periods of illness. Although there are many instances on record that describe how the companionship of a loyal, loving pet has helped an ailing person to get well, a case in 1984 illustrates this with particular drama.

An Englishman named Frank Mattingly was in a coma due to a mysterious illness. Loving words from his wife and other family members could not awaken him. All hope of his recovery was lost, when suddenly Frank whispered the name of his dog, Tipper.

The hospital staff agreed to have the dog brought to the hospital. Dogs, of course, were not allowed inside, so they led him to the roof of an adjacent building one floor below Frank's room. Frank's bed and all of his medical equipment were pushed toward the open window.

Tipper started barking and howling, and even tried to climb up a wall as if to get closer to Frank. At that point Frank awoke from his coma and started talking.

Everybody was amazed, none more so than Frank himself. "It was," he said, "as though I was brought back from the dead."

# Famous Dog Lovers

Although he owned no pets of his own, Cary Grant still had a soft spot in his heart for animals, especially dogs. One night on his way to a restaurant, he spotted a man walking a dog. The man, who had been drinking, was jerking the leash, causing the poor creature much distress. The more the dog yelped, the more the man pulled on the leash.

Maureen Donaldson, who was with Grant that evening, describes the incident in her autobiography, *An Affair to Remember: My Life with Cary Grant*:

> *"Look here," Cary said as he walked up to the man. "I will give you a hundred dollars right now if you will give me that dog."*
>
> *"You wanna buy my dog?" the man said woozily.*
>
> *"That's correct," Cary said, careful not to challenge the man on his treatment of the animal. This was strictly a transaction between two businessmen.*
>
> *"Well, I'll tell ya," the man said, weaving about while the dog still yelped. "This dog is worth two hundred dollars. Whaddya think about that?"*

"Why, you're absolutely right," Cary agreed. "I wouldn't want to cheat you!"

He reached into his wallet quickly, pulled out ten twenty-dollar bills and handed them to the man at the same moment he snatched the leash out of his hands. We were well on our way toward the restaurant before the man even realized what had happened.

"My God," Cary whispered. "What are we going to do with this mutt?"

"I don't know," I said, grabbing his hand, "but I love you."

"And what brought that on?" he said, genuinely confused.

"Doesn't matter," I said firmly. "But I love you."

"Good," he replied. "Then you find a home for this animal!"

# Chow Time for Elvis

Cary Grant was not, of course, the only celebrity who cared about dogs. Elvis owned a chow chow named Gitlow, and his affection and concern for the dog's well-being was clearly revealed when Gitlow was diagnosed with a critical kidney ailment. The nature of the illness was such that Gitlow couldn't be treated in Memphis, where Elvis lived, so he flew his beloved chow on his private plane to a special clinic in Boston. Unfortunately, the dog did not survive, and Elvis was devastated.

# More Famous Dog Lovers

In addition to Elvis and Cary Grant, other celebrities who have owned or own chow chows include Sally Struthers, Queen Victoria, former president Calvin Coolidge, Howard Baker and Heather Locklear. Perhaps it is the chow chow's endearing facial expression, caused by the unique furrows of skin and fur, that make it so appealing.

George Washington, Pablo Picasso, Robert De Niro,

Gloria Estefan, Richard Simmons, Darren McGavin, Don Johnson, Bobby Short and Eugene O'Neil owned or currently own Dalmatians.

Dalmatians are the tenth most popular breed among American dog owners, but their quick tempers and other personality foibles do not make them the ideal pet. Their popularity is largely due to the appealing way they've been portrayed by Disney in *101 Dalmatians*. The first version of this film was made in 1961, based on Dodie Smith's bestselling book published in 1956.

German shepherds reportedly make much better companions, mainly because they're loyal, devoted, responsible and love to work for their owners. Some famous shepherd owners include George Hamilton, Bob Hope, Jack Lalanne, Roy Rogers and former president Franklin D. Roosevelt.

Like people, however, they too can have unpleasant dispositions. Franklin Roosevelt had two German shepherds, Major and Meg, both of whom were prone to misbehaving in the most politically incorrect manner: Major bit Senator Hattie Caraway and England's Prime Minister James MacDonald; Meg committed what might be construed among politicians as a much lesser offense—she bit a journalist, Bess Furman.

Pablo Picasso, John Wayne, Clark Gable, Andy Warhol, Liz Smith, Errol Flynn and William Randolph Hearst owned dachshunds.

George and Barbara Bush, Fatty Arbuckle, Vicki Lawrence and Patrick Muldoon are some famous English springer spaniel owners.

Charles Schulz, Roger Staubach, Eva Gabor and Barry Manilow have owned beagles.

Golden retreivers are owned by Oprah Winfrey, Mary Tyler Moore, former president Gerald Ford, Jimmy Stewart, Bill Blass, Bob Newhart, Chevy Chase and Frank Gifford.

## It's For You, Spot

Thirty-three percent of dog owners talk to their pets on the phone or through the answering machine; but no pets have pagers, at least as of this writing.

# A Dog with a Freudian Bent

It would seem appropriate that the brilliant psychoanalyst Sigmund Freud would also have a brilliant dog. Wolf, a German shepherd, was indeed that. The dog could hail a cab. Well, sort of.

One day in Vienna, Wolf took off and got lost. Although the Freud family searched frantically for their pet's whereabouts, they could not find him.

Later that day, the dog turned up in a taxi, safe and sound. According to the cab driver, the dog had jumped into his vehicle and refused to move until the driver read his name and address on his collar tags. The cab driver drove him home, and the dog happily jumped out in front of his Freudian residence.

# Great Quotes About Dogs

*The great pleasure of a dog is that
you may make a fool of yourself with him
and not only will he not scold you, but
he will make a fool of himself too.*

—SAMUEL BUTLER

*To his dog, every man is Napoleon;
hence the constant popularity of dogs.*

—ALDOUS HUXLEY

*The dog is the god of frolic.*

—HENRY WARD BEECHER

# Running Scared

A frightened dog puts his tail between his legs because it cuts off the scent glands in its anal region, a very vulnerable part of the anatomy. "Since the anal glands carry personal scents that identify the individual dogs," writes Desmond Morris in *Dogwatching*, "the tail-between-the-legs action, is the canine equivalent of insecure humans hiding their faces."

# Dogs Were First in Space

In 1957, a Russian canine was the first living creature to go up in space.

# Kiss Me Canine

Next time your puppy licks your face, he might be looking for more than a kiss. In the wild, hungry pups too young to hunt for their own food lick the faces of their mothers, searching for food scraps. This action also triggers a reflex in the mother that causes her to regurgitate, giving the pups their meal.

# Why Do Dogs Eat So Fast?

It's another habit left over from the wild, where there was fierce competition for food. Not knowing when they would get their next meal, wild dogs ate as quickly and as much as they could before their food could be stolen by larger rivals like the hyena.

# Something to Chew On

Dogs love to chew on bones. It strengthens and cleans their teeth. But never give your dog poultry bones. They're soft, and could be swallowed whole and splinter inside your dog's stomach.

# Dogs That Smell for a Living

Dogs are commonly used to sniff out drugs at border checkpoints and other areas where drug smuggling occurs. But it's not an easy job to obtain. In fact, four out of five dogs fail drug-sniffing school. It's a talent that not all dogs possess.

## How They Do It

The sniffer dog is given the item to sniff, such as drugs or explosives. Instinctively, it connects the smell to the visual image. Then, at its master's command, it sniffs out the trail leading to the desired material.

## Just Rewards

When professional sniffers—dogs who graduate from sniffing school—successfully accomplish their task, they are usually rewarded with a little playtime. For instance, when a drug-sniffing dog sniffs out a package of marijuana, he will be allowed to play a game with the package. Work must always be interpreted by a dog as play.

# The Ancient Guard Dog—
# Or Three Heads Are
# Better Than One

In ancient Greek mythology, the three-headed hound Cerberus guarded the gates of hell, keeping the living out and, more importantly, the dead in.

# Vacationing Dogs

According to a survey by the American Animal Hospital Association, 53 percent of pet owners vacation or travel with their pets.

# The Dog Star

Sirius, the dog star, is the brightest star in the sky and was particularly important to the ancient Egyptians. Part of the constellation Canis Major, it rose over the horizon during the annual flood of the river Nile. This made the land fertile again, so the Egyptians worshiped this star for its life-giving properties.

It's called the "dog star" because it was said to have an influence on the canine race.

# The Hair of the Dog

Dogs are usually bred to help humans with hunting and herding, or for enjoyment of their personality and style. However, in Mexico, hairless dogs were bred and used as small space heaters.

Technically known as *cane nudo*, these dogs were brought from Africa in about 1600. They range in size from ten to sixteen inches and weigh between nine and

eighteen pounds. The only hair they have is on their heads. Their body temperature is very warm to the touch, about 102 degrees Fahrenheit, making them perfect bed companions for cold winter nights in the mountains of Mexico.

# Dogs at the Office

Mad Dogs & Englishmen, a New York advertising agency, allows employees to bring their dogs to work with them.

The agency was started by Nick Cohen, who brought his two dogs to the office to keep him company. The firm prospered, and as the number of employees grew, so did the number of pets. He now has twenty-five

employees, many of them dog lovers who bring their pets to work on alternate days. Cohen says, "The dogs help the creative environment. Clients like it, too. It makes us more memorable."

# The Original Purpose of Poodles

Usually, when you think of a poodle you think of a pampered, coddled creature with fancy grooming, but this breed of dog didn't always have it so good. In England, poodles were originally bred to hunt ducks and geese in muddy swamps.

# Dogs, a Good
# Source of Affection

Forty-eight percent of female dog owners rely more on their pet than a spouse or child for affection, compared to 38 percent of male pet owners.

# Cat of the Year Honor...
# Goes to a Dog

Ginny, a ten-year-old part-schnauzer, part-Siberian husky, won the Cat of the Year Award in November 1998. The annual honor, given by the Westchester Cat Show, in New York, usually goes to "a cat who displays unusual courage, determination, will to live or other special quality...."

But the judges were so impressed with Ginny's exploits that they bucked tradition and gave it to her.

Ginny roams the roads and alleys of her town and finds stray cats, especially those who are injured, hungry or just plain scared, and brings them to the comfort of her Long Island home.

Well, it's not exactly *her* home. It's the home of Ginny's owner, Philip Gonzalez, who also won a ribbon for his work in finding homes for the needy felines his pet dog sniffs out.

According to an *Associated Press* report, Mr. Gonzalez has placed hundreds of cats and himself has taken in a deaf cat, a one-eyed cat and a cat with no hind feet.

"Ginny," says Gonzalez, "prefers cats to dogs."

# Self-Sacrificing Dogs

As many dog lovers know, dogs can be incredibly generous and loving. A remarkable example of this concerns a German shepherd who gave its own life for its human family.

As a fire raged through the house, the dog covered a toddler with its own body. The dog died, but when the firefighters removed the dead dog's body, they were surprised to find the toddler still alive with only minor

injuries. Had it not been for the dog's heroic efforts, the toddler would have surely perished in the blaze.

# Health Tip

If you like to take your dog on long walks in the country, experts recommend that you put your pet on a medication called Interceptor, a pill given once a month that will prevent mosquito-carried heartworm as well as parasites such as roundworm, hookworm and whipworm.

This is an especially important measure to take to ensure your dog's health if you live in tropical areas, such as South Florida, where mosquitoes are found in annoying abundance.

# My Dog's an Angel

Many dog owners think dogs are angels—some literally. In *Animals as Teachers and Healers,* Susan Chernak McElroy recounts a spine-chilling tale of a collie that angelically appeared out of nowhere to lead a woman to safety.

The woman was in a hurry to get home and decided to take a shortcut through a park. Unbeknownst to her, the park was a hangout for unsavory characters

and an unsafe place for a woman to be walking alone at night.

"The collie ran up to the woman," writes McElroy, "assumed a perfect 'at heel' position and accompanied her into the park. The woman felt comforted by the presence of the huge dog, as it reminded her of a beloved collie who had been her childhood friend. Three times in the park that night, the woman was approached by rough-looking young men. Each time, the collie stepped out in front of her with a menacing stance." This forced the men to back off.

When she safely arrived at her apartment, she turned to thank the helpful dog, but it was nowhere to be seen. Like a guardian angel, it had vanished the minute the job was done.

# To Neuter or Not to Neuter

Neutering is a good idea for several reasons. Not only will you have a happier, healthier pet, you'll also help stem the tide of animal overpopulation.

Spayed and neutered pets are generally happier because they are free from sexual anxiety, and are therefore calmer and more content to stay at home. And if you have more than one pet, you'll find that they get along better.

In male dogs, neutering usually means a diminishing of aggressive behavior.

# Get That Dog a License

Your dog should have a license. If he runs off, not only will it be easier for someone who finds him to return him to you, but unlicensed dogs are "put to sleep" by animal control agencies sooner than dogs with license tags.

If you're away on vacation for a few days and your dog gets out of the backyard, the few extra days that a licensed dog is given in a shelter could save its life.

# Canine Company—
# But at What Price?

According to the Humane Society, you can expect to spend about one thousand dollars per year on your dog to keep him or her in tip-top shape.

That would include: feeding, $115 to $400 annually; adoption from pet shelter, $55; toys and grooming supplies, $160; vaccinations, $200 for the first year, $65 the following years; grooming, $50 per visit; boarding for a ten- to fourteen-day stay, $300; training, $50 to $100 annually; vet care, $135; and flea and tick care, $80 annually.

# Rent-a-Dog

If one thousand dollars a year is too much for you to spend on a dog, then you can always rent one; that is, if you live in Japan. In Japan, pet shops provide canine company for ten to twenty dollars an hour, depending on the size of the dog you desire.

# Training Tip

If you'd like to train your dog to give you his paw, just say, "Give me your paw," then tap on his leg or tickle it. When he picks up his paw, take it in your hand and praise him. Do this repeatedly until your dog responds promptly.

# Training Tip II

Applying a little gentle pressure on your dog's ear will help teach him to take an object in his mouth. Some of the world's greatest canine Frisbee catchers got started this way.

# What Should I Do If I Think a Dog Might Attack?

Never scream or run. Remain motionless, hands at your sides and avoid eye contact with the dog.

Keep still until the dog loses interest in you; then, slowly back away until he is out of sight.

If the dog attacks, "feed" him your jacket, purse, or anything that you can put between you and his mouth.

If you are knocked to the ground, curl into a ball with your hands over your ears and remain motionless. Try not to scream or roll around.

# Pet Cemetery

Americans spend a lot of money on their pets, even after they're dead. Pet cemeteries gross about $30 million annually, and the cost of burying your dog can range anywhere between several hundred and several thousand dollars, depending on how lavish a funeral setup you'd like.

At Pet's Rest Cemetery in Colma, California, for instance, burying a medium-sized pet in a pine box,

with a small redwood plaque costs, as of this writing, $600, including local pickup of the dog's body. For a custom casket with a granite headstone, figure on spending about $925. Annual maintenance is $30.

# There's No Place Like Home

While some owners prefer pet cemeteries as a place of rest, more than half of all pet owners bury their pet on family property.

# WANTED

The Humane Society offers up to $2,500 for information leading to the arrest and conviction of any wholesale dealer of dogs and cats who knowingly buys or otherwise procures stolen animals.

This group also offers up to $2,500 for information leading to the arrest and conviction of any person who organizes, promotes or officiates at dog fights.

# Smile!

The average dog has forty-two permanent teeth.

# Dogs Need You

An overabundance of dogs has resulted in a lot of homeless dogs. It is estimated that there are at least ten thousand cats and dogs born every day in the United States.

According to the American Society for the Prevention of Cruelty to Animals, even if every household adopted one of these pets, every American home would be filled in three years.

# A Cure for Yapping Dogs

If your dog is a yapper—and most smaller breeds are—a good cure is to raise your finger and encourage it to speak softer and softer until the dog earns a prize, such as a biscuit, a special treat or a hug.

Never, never hit a dog. Your tone of voice is sufficient to get your point across. Love and praise are more effective than physical force.

# Dogs with Muscle

Canine weight-hauling contests are held in some parts of the country. Competing dogs test their strength by pulling heavy loads.

According to *Dog Facts,* Bothell, Washington, hosts the World Championship Weight-Hauling Contest for Dogs. There are several categories, classified by weight. The greatest recorded load to have been shifted by a dog was 6,400.5 pounds. The champ? A 176-pound Saint Bernard named Ryettes Brandy Bear, who pulled approximately twenty-five times its own body weight on the first try.

# A Chilling Tail

Prince, a sad-eyed poodle mix, survived eighteen hours in a freezer with dozens of dead dogs.

On Mother's Day, 1997, Prince was hit by a car. "We brought him to our yard and petted him and thought maybe he would come back," said Ruben Majica, the dog's owner. "But he didn't. My kids were sick about it."

Animal Control officials thought he was dead, too,

and stored him in the deep freeze with other deceased dogs awaiting final disposal.

But Prince wasn't dead. When Earl Monroe, head of the agency, opened the freezer door the next day, Prince looked up and smiled at him. Monroe, who'd been on the job twenty-nine years, was shocked; this had never happened before.

Prince was listless for a while, but after he thawed out, he was fine.

# How Seeing-Eye Dogs Got the Job

Seeing-eye dogs perform an invaluable service. Ever wonder how they got the job?

Like many great discoveries, it occurred strictly by accident. In 1916, a doctor in Germany was walking a blind man through the streets near the hospital where he worked when he was called away on an emergency. He left his German shepherd in charge of the patient.

When the doctor returned, he was surprised and delighted that the dog had remained with the patient. He was so impressed with the dog's loyalty and obedience that he began a training program for dogs as guides for the blind.

German shepherds, Labrador retrievers and golden retrievers are chosen ahead of other breeds because of their size, love of work, ease of grooming and confident nature.

Although this is a modern-day example of how dogs came to be employed as guides, dogs have been of service throughout history.

The first person to use dogs as guides was a German king in 100 B.C. In another example, a fresco of a guide dog leading a blind man was discovered on the wall of a house in Pompeii, buried for centuries by the volcanic eruption in 79 A.D.

In 1927, a German shepherd named Buddy became the first trained guide dog in the United States.

# Seeing-Eye Dog and Owner Switch Roles

Dogs have remarkable powers of empathy and are known to take on sympathetic illnesses of their owners. One of the most moving examples of this concerns Emma, a black Labrador retriever, who has the distinction of being the oldest guide dog for the blind on record.

She belonged to Sheila Hocken of Stapleford, Nottinghamshire, England, who was born blind. Emma served her well until an operation restored Sheila's sight.

Ironically, Emma developed cataracts and not long after went blind herself. Sheila then became a guide for her guide dog. They happily switched roles until Emma's death at the ripe old age of seventeen on November 17, 1981.

Sheila later wrote a bestselling book about their life together called *Emma and I.*

# A "Hearing-Ear" Dog?

Dogs not only perform a valuable service for the blind, they are also employed by the deaf. "Hearing" dogs are the ears for their owners. They're trained to respond to various sounds, such as knocks on the door, the whistle of a teakettle or a ringing telephone. For a deaf person, the hearing dog becomes a critical ally that makes day-to-day living safer and happier.

Indeed, dogs are now employed to help all manner of handicapped individuals. Seizure-response dogs help people who have epileptic and other types of seizures. They are trained to get help or stay with the person during a seizure.

# Why Do Dogs Bury Bones?

A dog buries bones as a way of protecting leftovers. Commercial dog food is ill suited for this procedure, but bones endure. A doggy snack, then, is readily available at almost any time.

# The Dog Champ
of Dog Champs

It is the dog exhibitor's dream for their dog to win
one Challenge Certificate, or "CC" as dog fanciers call
them. U'Kwong King Solomon, a chow chow owned
and bred by Joan Egerton of Bramhall, Cheshire,
England, is the proud owner of an astonishing
seventy-eight certificates! This is the greatest number of CC's to be won by a British dog.

# High-Tech Cure
# for Dogs with Cancer

Gary and Michelle Hay of South Bend, Indiana, were heartbroken when their dog, Krueger, a six-year-old, 107-pound rottweiler, was diagnosed with cancer.

Not only were the Hays faced with the prospect of losing their beloved pet, but the community was in jeopardy of losing a valuable asset as well. Krueger is Indiana's only search-and-rescue dog certified by FEMA,

the Federal Emergency Management Agency. The cancer was in his paw, and amputation might have meant the end of Krueger's career.

But then one day, Gary was surfing the Internet and found Dr. Todd Jackson, a veterinarian at the University of Cincinnati. Jackson suggested that Krueger undergo radiation therapy, a cancer treatment usually reserved for humans, at the school's Veterinary Cancer Control Program. This was a welcome alternative to amputation, so Krueger underwent radiation therapy fifteen times in a three-week period during the spring of 1997. The treatment worked. A subsequent checkup showed that the dog's paw was cancer-free.

"We are providing medical treatments to our animal patients similar to treatment provided to people," said Dr. David Denman, associate professor of radiation oncology and director of the Veterinary Cancer Control Program, quoted in an article published in *The San Diego Union-Tribune.* "I'm not aware of any other medical school in the United States that has human machines just for veterinary patients."

The program benefits about thirty animals a year, but the knowledge gleaned from these cases helps doctors learn more about cancer treatment for humans.

"The main difference in treating cancer in dogs is that more information can be recorded in less time," Denman said. "One year in a dog's life is equivalent to five, six or seven years in a human's life."

# Are Dogs More Reliable Than Cats?

Seventy percent of dog owners expect their dog to come to their rescue when they're in distress compared to only 31 percent of cat owners.

# Dog Defined

One of the most charming and heartfelt comments ever made about man's best friend was written by Ambrose Bierce, who defined the dog as "a kind of additional or subsidiary deity designed to catch the overflow and surplus of the world's worship."

# A Final Tribute

Yes, dogs are our heroes. If anyone disagrees with this, they need only look at the statue of Balto, the sled dog who led one of twenty-two dog teams across treacherous terrain to bring an antitoxin to a city in Alaska that was fighting off a diphtheria epidemic.

The statue stands in New York's Central Park and bears the inscription: "Dedicated to the indomitable spirit of the sled dogs that relayed antitoxin six hundred

miles over rough ice, treacherous waters, through arctic blizzards from Nemana to the relief of stricken Nome in the winter of 1925. Endurance, Fidelity, Intelligence."

Long live the dog!

# The D.O.G. Man's Best Friend

# Works Cited

Associated Press. "Freed From Freezer, a 'Dead' Dog Thaws Out Alive." *The San Diego-Union Tribune,* 21 Aug., 1997.

Bardens, Dennis. *Psychic Animals: A Fascinating Investigation of Paranormal Behavior.* New York: Barnes & Noble, 1987.

Condax, Delano Kate. *Why Does My Dog Do That?!* Emmaus, Penn: Rodale Press, 1994.

Dodman, Nicholas. *Tales, Treatment and the Psychology of Dogs.* New York: Bantam Books, 1996.

Fogle, Bruce. *The Encyclopedia of the Dog.* New York: Dorling Kindersley, 1995.

Friend, Tim. "Dog Domestication Dates to Early Man." *USA Today.* 1 Aug., 1997.

MacDonald, Maureen, and William Royce. *An Affair to Remember: My Life with Cary Grant*. New York: Putnam, 1989.

McElroy, Chernak Susan. *Animals as Teachers and Healers*. New York: Ballantine Books, 1997.

Morris, Desmond. *Dogwatching*. New York: Crown Publishers, 1986.

Palika, Liz. *The German Shepherd: An Owner's Guide to a Happy and Healthy Pet*. New York: Howell Book House, 1995.

Palmer, Joan. *Dog Facts*. New York: Barnes & Noble, 1991.

Starr, Cindy. "Human-Type Therapy Gives Pets with Cancer a Fighting Chance." *The San Diego Union-Tribune*. (Scripps Howard News Service), 17 June 1997: E3.

Van Housen, Caty. "The Long Hot Summer: Lazy Days Pose Special Dangers to Pets; Some Safety Tips." *The San Diego-Union Tribune:* 24 June 1997: E4.

Wade, Nicholas. "Dog Has Been Man's Best Friend for Longer Than First Thought." *New York Times* News Service. 13 June 1997.

# Resources for Dog Lovers

**American Kennel Club (AKC)**
5580 Centerview Dr., Ste. 200
Raleigh, NC 27606
919-233-9767
There is a dog show every week somewhere in the United States; for show information, contact the AKC.

**American Animal Hospital Association (AAHA)**
12575 W. Bayard Ave.
Lakewood, CO 80228
303-986-2800
*www.healthypet.com*

**American Society for the Prevention of Cruelty to Animals (ASPCA)**
424 E. 92nd St.
New York, NY 10128-6804
*www.aspca.org*

**Humane Society**
Contact the local Humane Society in your area or visit their Web site at:
*www.humanesociety.org*

**North American Police Work Dog Association (NAPWDA)**
4222 Manchester Ave.
Perry, OH 44081
*www.napwda.com*

**Internet Sites**

**Dog Owner's Guide**
*www.canismajor.com/dog/ guide.html*

**Pet Placement Page**
*www.u.arizona.edu-rperu*